Cats

vmb
PUBLISHERS

CONTENTS

1
The coat of the Persian cat is officially recognized
in a multitude of colors.

2-3
Sleeping is one of kitty's favorite pastimes.

TEXT
FLAVIA CAPRA

GRAPHIC DESIGN
PAOLA PIACCO

INTRODUCTION

The American writer and humorist Oliver Herford – born in the UK and known as the Oscar Wilde "from across the pond" – once wrote: "Observing a cat is rather like viewing the creation of a work of art." One can only agree!

Whatever its breed, this small domestic feline exudes an irresistible charm: even those who are not particularly fond of this species admire its beauty.

People either love cats or detest them: there's no half way. Fortunately the number of those who appreciate their company is enormous – and growing. Because puss demands so little attention, she has become the ideal companion.

4-5
The coat of these adorable kittens features the classic tabby design, with stripes and fantastic arabesques.

Although four thousand years have gone by since this feline became domesticated, her independent character is by no means subdued: the cat continues to be a free spirit. You can't possess her: at most, it is she who possesses you. In fact, this small household creature can turn out to be a real tyrant!

There's no point in trying to educate your cat, or in imparting orders: kitty will never obey you – her reputation is at stake! You'll have to use guile. If she's clearly about to misbehave, your only option is to distract her from her intentions by playing with her, or by offering her some delicious morsel of food.

On the other hand, you must admit that the little rebel does have other virtues:

6-7
The way cats hold their tails and ears is indicative of their state of mind, and of any uneasiness.

8-9
The narrower the pupil is, the more accurate the cat's perception of depth.

she's affectionate, cuddly, even loyal – but she'll never be submissive, never a slave to mankind. In any case, a cat's loyalty and affection must be earned day by day. Nothing will induce her to stay in a home where she feels unloved; but by treating her with sensitivity and respect you will secure a sincere relationship that will bind the two of you for a lifetime. Incidentally, a cat has seven lives!

Chapter 1

THE STORY OF BREED SELECTION

10
The Siamese cat has a triangular head, large ears and an elongated body.

FOLLOWING THE FIRST CAT SHOW IN HISTORY – ORGANIZED BY HARRISON WILLIAM WEIR IN 1871 AT LONDON'S CRYSTAL PALACE – THE PUBLIC AT LARGE STARTED TO PAY MORE ATTENTION TO THIS SMALL HOUSEHOLD FELINE, WHICH HAD HITHERTO ENJOYED LITTLE CONSIDERATION, BEING OVERSHADOWED BY MAN'S TRADITIONAL FRIEND: THE DOG.

PEOPLE STARTED TO NOTICE THAT CATS ARE NOT DISTINGUISHED MERELY BY THEIR COATS OF DIFFERENT LENGTH AND COLOR, BUT ALSO BY A VARIETY OF SOMATIC AND MORPHOLOGICAL TRAITS.

SO BREEDS BEGAN TO BE IDENTIFIED, OWING IN PARTICULAR TO THE PATIENT SELECTION WORK OF A FEW CAT-LOVERS WHO, DESPITE THEIR LACK OF EXPERTISE AND KNOWLEDGE OF GENETICS, MANAGED TO ESTABLISH SOME OF THEIR CHARACTERISTICS.

EXOTIC CATS ARRIVED ON BRITISH TERRAIN WITH DIPLOMATS AND ARMY WORKERS RETURNING FROM ASSIGNMENTS ABROAD: FOR EXAMPLE, THE SIAMESE CAT, ORIGINATING FROM AND NAMED AFTER THE ANCIENT KINGDOM OF SIAM, PRESENT-DAY THAILAND. THESE FELINES ARE SLENDER AND IVORY IN COLOR, WITH MAGNIFICENT BLUE EYES, AND STRANGELY-COLORED EXTREMITIES (EARS, MUZZLE, PAWS AND TAIL).

The Abyssinian is a feline species originating from Ethiopia, historically called Abyssinia, whence the name.

12-13
The Turkish Angora cat is characterized by a long, silky coat, and a vivacious, communicative and sociable nature.

On the other hand, the Turkish angora cat is characterized by its flowing, long-haired coat, while the Abyssinian cat, brought to the UK by an army colonel at the end of the Ethiopian war, has a short, glossy, silky coat that is both exotic and stunning in appearance: each hair is traversed by different-colored bands.

And so it was that the Angora, British, European, Siamese, Burmese and Abyssinian breeds began to be favored by cat lovers and take the lead in cat shows, which had in the meantime become popular in the United States and Europe.

At a certain point, however, cat breeding took two different routes: certain breeds were kept as found in nature; others were modified by breeders who, for the purpose of fixing distinctive features, enthusiastically experimented with crossbreeding to obtain their objectives, sometimes taking particular characteristics to extremes.

Among the selected breeds are the Norwegian Forest Cat, the Maine Coon and the Siberian, all originating from the countries they are named after. Nature has endowed them with long-haired, flowing coats to protect them from the rigid climate and long winters of their homelands. That is their only common characteristic: in every other way their physical appearance is very different.

The Turkish Angora and the Turkish Van, both long-haired varieties, are originally from Turkey and have not been subjected to modifications; over the years, their breeders have merely indulged in the whim of extending the range of colors and patterns of their coat, without changing their overall appearance.

14
The ears of the Maine Coon are very large, and placed high up on the head.

15
The Maine Coon is one of the largest feline breeds: an adult male can weigh up to 19.8 lbs (9 kg).

16
The Siberian is a strong and extremely agile cat.

17
Norwegian cats have a rectangular body, a triangular head
and a straight profile.

Certain selected breeds maintain their original colors, such as the Russian Blue, the Chartreux and the Korat. What these cats have in common is the color of their coat, which has to be a delicate shade of blue-gray in order to be accepted; but the texture of their fur and their somatic and morphological traits are markedly different.

18
Until they are one year old, Russian Blue kittens can have a faintly striped coat.

19
Russian Blue cats have a blue coat with gray nuances.

20
British Longhair cats descend from the British Shorthair breed,
whose gentle nature they have inherited.

21
British Shorthair cats have large, round, extremely expressive eyes,
and coats that come in many colors.

While certain varieties are noted and selected for their outstanding beauty, others appeal for their curious distinguishing characteristics, as is the case of the Devon Rex, a breed with short, thick, wavy fur that was found in an abandoned mine in Devon, England. Its coat is truly unusual and its somatic traits – particularly its high, pronounced cheek bones, short muzzle and very large ears – lend this cat an elfish look. Carlo Rambaldi, the well-known special effects creator for the cinema, winner

22
Large ears and a startled expression are among the characteristics of the Devon Rex.

23
Devon Rex: this cat is the result of a spontaneous genetic mutation, selected in England in the 1950s.

of three Academy Awards, is said to have
been inspired by this breed for his legendary character, ET.

Mother Nature used boundless imagination in coloring, decorating and curling feline coats; she had fun bending their ears forward (Scottish Fold) and backward (American Curl); lopping off their tails (Manx); or curling them (Japanese Bobtail and Kurilian Bobtail).

24-25
Back-curled ears are one of the distinguishing features of the American Curl.

Breeders' creativity did the rest. Starting off with cats of average build and somatic traits, through selection they arrived at individuals with extreme characteristics, such as ever longer tubular bodies; long legs; perfectly triangular heads; straight or even convex profiles; long, thin tails: features currently found in Siamese, Balinese, Oriental and Javanese cats.

26-27
The Balinese cat has similar somatic and morphological traits to the Siamese cat: they only differ in the length of their coat.

27
The Oriental cat has a tubular-shaped body, long slender legs, a triangular head, and large ears.

Meanwhile, lovers of rounded shapes managed to create a feline with a squat body, short legs and a perfectly round head. A very short nose with a pronounced stop and small ears complete the profile of the Persian and of the Exotic Shorthair. The standard for the two breeds is the same; only their coats differ: long, thick, abundant in the Persian and short, but again very thick and voluminous in the Exotic.

28
This lovely young ginger Persian looks misleadingly sulky, when in fact Persians are very sweet-natured.

29
The Persian Cat's coat is long, thick and silky. Nowadays its recognized colors are innumerable.

30
The Exotic Shorthair is none other than a short-haired Persian, and has the same coat.

31
Only females have tricolor coats: pictured here is an Exotic Blue cream and white specimen.

Among the breeds that have always fascinated throngs of breeders we mustn't forget the Sacred Cat of Burma, with its long, silky ivory-colored coat, darker-colored extremities and its distinctive characteristic: legendary white gloves. Its magnetic, sapphire-blue eyes bewitch even the most indifferent onlookers, and myth mingles with reality in the story of its birth or creation.

Another variety resulting from a carefully engineered selection is the Ragdoll, so called – they say – because of its faculty to relax completely when picked up. Like the Burmese cat, the Ragdoll has an ivory-colored coat with darker extremities and stunning blue eyes. The two breeds differ only in their size and in the distribution of the white markings (which can be absent in the Ragdoll).

32
Ragdoll cats have touches of white on their feet, while the rest of their body has a Himalayan pattern.

33
The Sacred Cat of Burma has an ivory-colored body; darker mask, ears, legs and tail; and white "gloves."

34
A beautiful close-up of a Sphynx, showing this breed's
typical wrinkles.

35
The Sphynx, also known as the "naked cat,"
is completely hairless.

Long-haired, short-haired... each category has its supporters: according to some, in order to distinguish itself from the common housecat, an aristocratic cat must be long-haired; for others, a "true feline" must have a short-haired coat.

But there is a third possibility. In recent years, in fact, a new feline category has made its debut on the pedigree catwalk: the naked cat! In all truth, the absence of hair in the domestic cat is not really a novelty, having been noted already at the turn of the twentieth century; but hardly anyone had considered selecting it. This phenomenon has only recently attracted the attention of cat lovers and as a result the Sphynx has now become a full-fledged member of the large family of purebred cats.

Another recently selected hairless variety is the Peterbald, a cat whose aero-dynamic body, while resembling that of the Siamese, is completely naked.

Many breeders have long dreamed of reproducing the coats of large felines on domestic cats. Through a combination of genetic studies and breeders' passion it has been possible to conserve natural gene pools while "creating" miniature marvels, such as the Egyptian Mau and the Ocicat, both of whom flaunt a perfect leopard-like spotted coat. But the real marvel – the breed that most closely resembles the wild feline – is undoubtedly the Bengal: selected in the United States in the 1960s, it perfectly reproduces the ocelot's fur.

36-37
A lot of selection and imagination on the breeders' part went into the spotted fur of the Bengal Cat.

Today, feline associations worldwide recognize a multitude of breeds, each of them meticulously described in their respective standards. All tastes are catered for!

However, we mustn't forget that even the humble housecat has contributed – to no small degree – to the selection of many of the varieties recognized today; and that it is among these very same common felines that judges sometimes discover the most beautiful specimens of the European breed, native to the Old Continent.

38-39
The European is the Old Continent's native cat, selected from the common housecat.

Chapter 2

EARLY STEPS:
THE RULES OF LIFE

THE SHE-CAT'S GESTATION PERIOD GENERALLY LASTS BETWEEN 62 AND 65 DAYS, ALTHOUGH KITTENS HAVE BEEN KNOWN TO BE BORN AFTER 59 DAYS, AND EVEN AFTER 70. KITTENS AT BIRTH WEIGH ON AVERAGE BETWEEN 2.82 AND 4.23 OUNCES (80–120 G), AND HAVE A WEIGHT RANGE OF BETWEEN 2.11 AND 5.29 OUNCES (60–150 G). THEIR WEIGHT DEPENDS ON VARIOUS FACTORS, SUCH AS THEIR BREED (A MAINE COON IS DECIDEDLY LARGER THAN A SINGAPURA); GENDER (FEMALES ARE SMALLER THAN MALES); NUMBER OF KITTENS IN THE LITTER AND, LAST BUT NOT LEAST, THE MOTHER'S DIET DURING HER PREGNANCY.

ONCE THE GESTATION PERIOD IS OVER, THE SHE-CAT WILL LOOK FOR A SAFE, DRY, PROTECTED PLACE TO GIVE BIRTH TO HER OFFSPRING. SOMETIMES HER SEARCH FOR THE RIGHT PLACE WILL START MANY DAYS IN ADVANCE, AND SHE MIGHT CHANGE HER MIND SEVERAL TIMES BEFORE FINDING A DESTINATION THAT SHE CONSIDERS IDEAL.

40
A very protective mother, the she-cat keeps her kittens under constant supervision.

When the last kitten of the litter has seen the light, mother cat lies down, relaxed, embracing her little ones to keep them warm, licking them repeatedly to stimulate them, and pushing them gently with her head, inviting them to attach themselves to her teats to suckle. A new-born kittens' body temperature is rather low, around 98.6°F (37°C), while that of a healthy adult feline should be 101.3°F (38.5°C): therefore the little ones must be kept constantly warm, avoiding sudden changes in temperature which could have lethal consequences.

Kittens are born deaf, with their eyes still closed; only their sense of smell is well-developed, enabling the little ones to recognize their mother and brothers immediately. Owing to this – minutes after its birth, and nuzzled by its mother – each kitten find its way to a teat, attaches itself and suckles its mother's colostrum. It contains a wealth of antibodies which strengthen the little ones' immune system. Only after this period does milk actually come in.

42-43
If they are not removed from their mother, kittens will nurse even after they are four weeks old.

In the earliest days of their lives, kittens are totally dependent on their mother. She knows this very well, and never leaves them unattended except for the few minutes it takes for her to eat. Throughout this period, kittens attach themselves frequently and voraciously to their mother's teats, stimulating the milk supply by kneading the sides of her nipples with alternate movements of their little paws, and accompanying each feed with their sonorous "purr-purr".

The mother cat, happy and proud of her litter, lies on her side with her eyes closed, letting her kittens take their fill of the warm milk that springs from her teats, warming them with her body, and joining in with the purring concert.

44-45
Kittens open their eyes after their tenth day of life, but don't see well at this stage.

46
Up to their third week of age, the kittens' activity is limited to nursing and sleeping.

47
At birth, the she-cat licks her little ones to keep them clean.

In their first eight days the little ones grow on average 0.35–0.52 ounces a day (10–15 g), and by the end of the first week their weight has usually doubled.

Each kitten lays claim to its own nipple, which it identifies by its unique scent, and defends from its brothers' attack with vigorous paw-blows and intense meowing.

Kittens open their eyes during their first 8 and 10 days, but at this stage can only distinguish shadows; day after day their sight improves, and images become clear when they are two weeks old. Together with their eyesight, their hearing begins to work, becoming finer and finer. In this period, for roughly three weeks, the mother cat devotes herself ceaselessly to her offspring, nursing her kittens lovingly, and keeping them clean by licking them regularly all over.

After the third week, the little ones begin to leave their den and explore their surroundings under the constant supervision of their mother: she allows them to toddle here and there, without letting them out of sight. If a kitten strays too far or approaches a source of danger, mother cat takes over immediately, calling out

to it with particular intensity, and steering it towards the cat bed with her paw as if to show it the way – just as a mother does when she takes her child by the hand.

48-49
When they reach one month of age, kittens start to venture away from their nesting area.

49
When around three weeks old, the little ones start exploring their surroundings under their mother's gaze.

50-51
Playing is an ideal work-out for the kitten's
sinuous, flexible muscles.

51
A butterfly has captured this kitten's attention:
although she's playing, she's already trying to
catch it.

In cases of disobedience or of excessive distance, the she-cat adopts a different technique: she picks up her kitten by the scruff, and carries it back to their den. She does this with extraordinary delicacy, without harming the skin or muscles of the little one's tiny neck.

Little teeth begin to show around the

third week, and this is the time for the mother cat to start weaning her kittens, teaching them to eat from the bowl, or bringing them small scraps of meat torn from her prey.

As the days go by, Mama Cat's teachings become increasingly specific and detailed: she passes down to her offspring the principles she learnt, in turn, from her own mother, using the same instincts and intuition that Mother Nature has given her.

52
Around the age of four weeks, kittens explore their surroundings.

53
On their earliest escapades the little ones move rather clumsily.

Cats who live out of doors, and don't have access to a litter box, urinate and defecate in the sand or ground, after digging a hole, then cover everything up carefully.

But if the mother is a housecat who has access to a litter box, she leads her kittens to discover this secluded corner, reserved to kitty "business," and trains them to use it. Cats are clean creatures, and kittens soon learn not to relieve themselves where they shouldn't.

By playing with her little ones, Mama Cat teaches them to hunt and use ambush, attack and prey-immobilization techniques. These will be fine-tuned over time, through experience and necessity.

At first, the mother cat uses whatever natural material she can find – leaves, bits of wood, pieces of paper or other light material – that she can easily animate by lifting it in the air with her paws.

The kittens take part in this sport: clumsy at first, they become more and more agile, attentive, involved, until they start stealing each other's prey, growling and hissing to defend their trophies.

It's but a small step from simulation to fact: small mice, lizards, birds and insects are the ritual victims that Mama Cat brings to her little ones; she deposits them, still alive, at their feet to check their learning progress, while keeping in the vicinity to prevent the prey from escaping.

The kittens' instinct is strong, and generally a few "paws-on" lessons are enough to learn all the tricks.

By the time they are three months old, the kittens have learned from their mother all the survival basics: they are weaned, independent "teenagers," ready to leave their nest and try their wings.

54
A field can conceal lots of small prey: crickets, grasshoppers, butterflies, ants…

55
A tree is just the thing for exercising… even upside down.

56
Going up is much easier than coming down… but it's only a matter of practice!

56-57
A wind-shaken twig can become a small victim, to be caught and immobilized.

Chapter 3

FELINE
INSTINCT

WITH A SUPPLE BODY, MUSCLES OF STEEL, AND THE REFLEXES OF A 328 FT (100 M) SPRINT ATHLETE POISED AT THE STARTING BLOCKS, CATS ARE PERFECT MACHINES. YOU WOULDN'T THINK SO WHEN OBSERVING A CAT LOUNGING IN THE SUN, BUT ALL HER SENSES ARE EXTREMELY SHARP. HER ULTRA-FINE HEARING PERCEIVES SOUNDS AT VERY HIGH FREQUENCIES; HER EYESIGHT IS EXCEPTIONAL, ESPECIALLY AT NIGHT-TIME, WHEN HER PUPILS EXPAND AND CAPTURE EVEN THE SLIGHTEST DETAILS. HER WHISKERS ACT LIKE RADAR, GUIDING HER IN PITCH DARKNESS SO THAT SHE CAN AVOID OBSTACLES; HER SENSE OF SMELL IS HIGHLY DEVELOPED, AND CAN EASILY COMPETE WITH A DOG'S. SHE HAS AN AGILE, FLEXIBLE BODY, CAPABLE OF JUMPING HIGH, RUNNING FAST, CLIMBING TREES AND PLAYING. THE LATTER IS VERY IMPORTANT: IT'S A WAY FOR ADULT CATS TO LET OFF STEAM, RELAX AND RELIEVE TENSION; AND FOR ELDERLY CATS TO KEEP FIT AND AGILE.

58
Cats are also very playful, and their antics express their different states of mind.

60
Beautiful, expressive, mysterious: cat eyes have always symbolized charm and elegance.

61
In the same way as humans, cats have binocular vision: this enables them to perceive distance.

By observing cats at play we can gain insight into their hunting techniques: they hide, lie in ambush, challenge each other, lock in wrestling, nibbling each other's paws, muzzle and any other parts that lie within reach of their mouths; they play with their companions' tails, and with any moving object. A blade of grass or a wind-blown leaf is enough to draw their attention and engage them extensively. These activities also help to keep their muscles well-toned, and train their eyesight to detect the slightest movement; and improve their reflexes, which are already highly developed in this species. By challenging their companions in play, cats learn new defence and attack techniques, and test their mettle.

62-63
Climbing trees: not just for fun, but also to sharpen their claws.

64 and 65
Generally speaking, cats hunt at nighttime, and enjoy roaming in daytime.

66-67
Lurking in the grass, this young cat is watching her prey, and preparing for the final attack.

Cats adopt two basic techniques to capture their prey: attack and ambush.

When attacking, the feline squats and, watching the prey's every movement, moves slowly and silently towards it; now the cat pauses, calculating the exact distance; then, with a measured leap, she pounces on her victim.

When lying in wait, puss lurks in a corner, unseen, waiting patiently for her prey to appear, then bounds towards her unfortunate target.

She can sit for hours by a pond, immobile, observing the depths of the water until a fish, oblivious of danger, swims to the edge. At that point, in a flash, the cat lashes out and hooks her prey.

Indeed, as well as a hunter, the cat can reveal herself to be an excellent... fisherman!

Her front paws have retractable claws that can even capture flying targets, while very thick, elastic paw-pads enable kitty to approach her victim soundlessly. When lying in wait, she keeps her back legs – which are longer than her front legs, and very muscular – flexed under her body, ready to pounce for the final attack.

68-69
With a predatory instinct that is ever alert, nothing escapes the eyes of a cat.

Despite her great speed, the house-cat is not a long-distance runner: for this reason you rarely see her chasing her prey for long. If her attack fails she prefers to withdraw with nonchalance, feigning indifference. Cats are very touchy: they don't like to make a bad impression!

If her hunt is instead successful and she has captured her prey, she bites the nape of its neck, breaking its backbone to immobilize it.

70-71 and 71
Cats use classic feline hunting techniques, such as stalking and lying in ambush.

72
Mama-cat returns to her kittens with her prey dangling in her mouth.

73
A successful hunt: this unfortunate mouse has ended up under kitty's claws.

The most frequent victims are small birds, mice, lizards, leverets, snakes, small insects. In most cases, cats kill their prey, or abandon it; but a housecat might bring it home as a trophy. Don't ignore her present: she will be mortally offended!

Felines are by nature solitary wanderers, except when they live in colonies: generally speaking they like to patrol the territory they have conquered on their own, defending it obstinately, and engaging in fights. During her explorations, a cat will sometimes find herself in really dangerous situations: that's when her sixth sense – balance – comes into play.

74-75
Cats have the skill of tightrope-walkers, the
grace of acrobats, and don't suffer from vertigo.

75
Lithe backbones and flexible muscles enable
cats to leap accurately.

With her supple, muscular body, kitty can perform the most daring feats – such as walking on the edge of railings, or on narrow roof ledges, like a skilled tight-rope artist; or climb to dizzy heights, without the least sign of vertigo or hesitation. This capacity derives from a sensory system residing in the cat's inner ear, controlling her balance: this is the vestibular apparatus and it is particularly

well-developed in the domestic feline.

It must be said: cats possess the ability and precision of tightrope walkers and their tails become the perfect balance-pole in case of need.

If, for example, a cat should fall upside-down from a great height, she can to turn herself around mid-fall and so land on her feet.

Lurking in the vineyard, this puss patiently waits for an unknowing bird.

77
Nothing escapes kitty's attentive gaze, as she hides behind the door.

As well as being a skilled hunter, puss is also very curious, and will snoop around any hiding place, nook and cranny, even at the risk of getting herself into trouble. She is famed for being fearless, when in fact she is a veritable scaredy-cat: sometimes an unusual sound or unexpected movement will be enough to send her scurrying away into hiding.

While the perfection of her antics is undisputed, kitty's extreme creativity can sometimes make her look like a clown: but isn't this one of her great charms?

The proverbial elegance and grace of her movements; her magnetic gaze and independent spirit; her capacity to pull through on any occasion, have won the heart of her admirers, for whom the cat is truly irresistible – the perfect creature, from every point of view.

INDEX

PHOTO CREDITS

AUTHOR

A true cat lover, **Flavia Capra** has learned to understand their nature, vices and virtues, in the process turning her passion into a profession. She obtained a license to judge international cat shows and began collaborating with major newspapers in Italy and abroad, eventually landing a position as an editorial director. Currently she works for the Associazione Nazionale Felina Italiana (ANFI - the Italian National Cat Association), the only association recognized by the Italian Ministry of Agriculture, Food and Forestry, where she is involved in the registration of cat breeds in the Italian genealogical registers. She is the author of "Super Cats", White Star Publishers.

VMB Publishers® is a registered trademark
property of De Agostini Libri S.p.A.

© 2013 De Agostini Libri S.p.A.
Via G. da Verrazano, 15
28100 Novara, Italy
www.whitestar.it - www.deagostini.it

Translation: Contextus s.r.l., Pavia (Sarah Jane Webb)
Editing: Contextus s.r.l., Pavia

ISBN: 978-88-540-2291-1
1 2 3 4 5 6   17 16 15 14 13

Printed in China